A Rollick of Recorders

A ROLLICK OF RECORDERS

OR OTHER INSTRUMENTS

❀ ❀ ❀

Thirteen Popular Colonial Tunes Set for Trio

❀ ❀ ❀

By Herbert Watson

THE COLONIAL WILLIAMSBURG FOUNDATION

Williamsburg, Virginia

Seventh Printing, 1995

LIBRARY OF CONGRESS CATALOGING-IN-PUBLICATION DATA

Watson, Herbert, 1941–
  A rollick of recorders, or other instruments.

  "Sources of the music": The dancing-master, The beggar's opera, Pills
to purge melancholy, and The compleat tutor for the flute.
  CONTENTS: The galloping nag.—The parson among the peas.—Drive
the cold winter away.—[etc.]
  1. Wind trios (3 recorders), Arranged. I. Title.
M358.W3R6   788'.53'523   75–12728
ISBN 0–87935–029–6

CONTENTS

SOURCES OF THE MUSIC

Playford, *The Dancing-Master* Tunes 1, 3, 4, 7, 8, 9, 11, and 13

The Dancing-Master: Vol. the first. Or, Directions for Dancing Country-Dances, with the Tunes to each Dance, for the Treble-Violin. The 18th Edition, . . . London: Printed by W. Pearson, and sold by Edward Midwinter . . . and John Young . . . [1725?]. (The first edition, volume 1 only, was published under the title *The English Dancing-Master*. London: J. Playford, 1651.)

Gay, *The Beggar's Opera* Tunes 5, 6, and 10

John Gay. *The Beggar's Opera, as it is acted at the Theatre-Royal in Lincolns-Inn Fields. The 3rd edition. With the Ouverture in Score, the Songs, and Basses (the Ouverture and Basses compos'd by Dr. Pepusch).* London: Printed for J. Watts, 1729.

D'Urfey, *Pills to Purge Melancholy* Tune 2

Wit and Mirth: or Pills to Purge Melancholy. Edited by Thomas D'Urfey. With an introduction by Cyrus L. Day. 6 vols. in 3. New York: Folklore Library Publishers, 1959. (A facsimile reproduction of the 1876 reprint of the original edition of 1719–20.)

Johnson, *Compleat Tutor for the Flute* Tune 12

The Compleat Tutor for the Flute. Containing the best and Easiest Instructions for Learners to obtain a Proficiency. To which is added a Choice Collection of the most celebrated Italian, English, and Scotch Tunes Curiously adapted to that Instrument. London: J. Johnson [no date but earlier than 1740].

PREFACE

THE PIECES in this collection have been arranged for the instrument that in the eighteenth century was known as the English flute or common flute. We know it as the recorder, and it has regained much of its former popularity, being once more available in different sizes just as it was when this advertisement appeared in the *Virginia Gazette*, Williamsburg's weekly paper, of November 29, 1770:

. . . to be SOLD at the POST OFFICE in Williamsburg . . . Instructions for the violin and flute . . . *German* and common flutes, of different sizes. . . .

From documentary records we know that music for flutes—both the transverse or German variety and the end-blown English kind, the recorder—was sold at other stores as well as at the Post Office. But we do not know anything about the music itself. A number of method books and collections of popular tunes published in London and other music centers of Europe could be bought by colonial music lovers, however. I have drawn on four of these. Playford's *Dancing-Master* and D'Urfey's *Pills to Purge Melancholy* contain an abundance of tunes that our colonial forebears used for light-hearted musicmaking. And inhabitants of Williamsburg would have been especially familiar with songs from *The Beggar's Opera*, which was performed in the colonial capital several times.

We hope that modern players will revive the eighteenth-century custom of playing these pieces with whatever instruments are at hand. I have set them for three sizes of recorder (soprano, alto, and tenor) and have used the clef and ranges familiar to recorder players; note especially the treble clef in the soprano line, indicating that it is to be played an octave higher. But the pieces will easily fit the registers of many other instruments, and might also be adapted for keyboard instruments. If only two players are present, the melody can be combined with one of the other two lines, preferably the bottom one, to produce a duet.

The original tunes contained no tempo or dynamic markings, and I have only indicated general markings, which are to be taken lightly. Phrasings occurring in the top line are in the originals and have been paralleled in the lower two lines. Other than that I have not added any phrasing.

For their help and encouragement I extend my thanks to James S. Darling, music consultant for Colonial Williamsburg; Charles Hardin and John Barrows, my colleagues of the Music Teacher's Room in the Historic Area; and John C. Moon, director of the Colonial Williamsburg Fife and Drum Corps.

1. THE GALLOPING NAG

Playford, *The Dancing-Master*

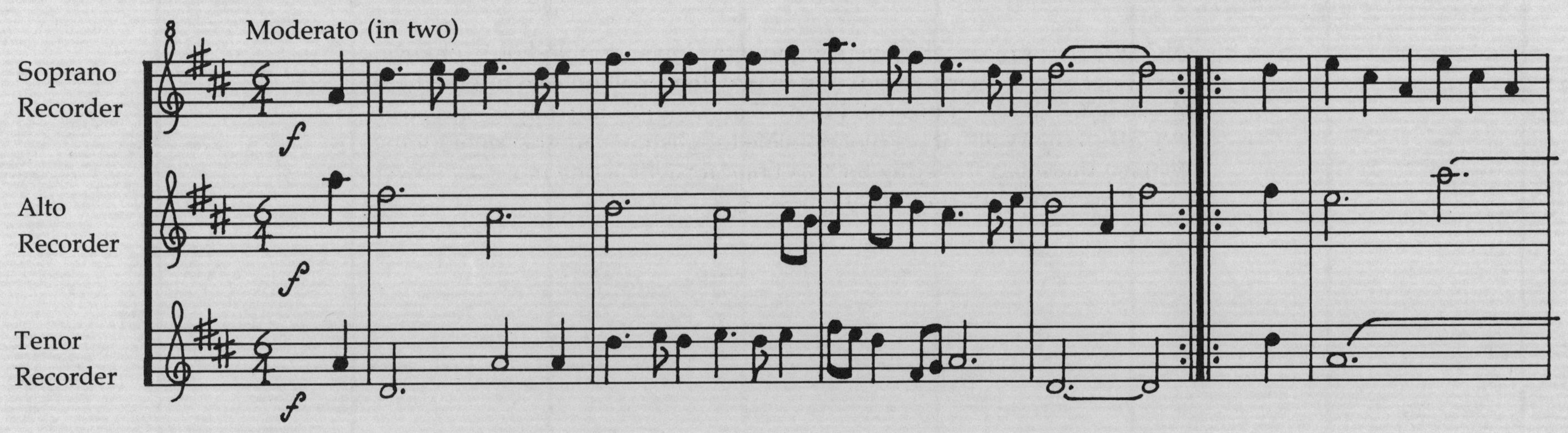

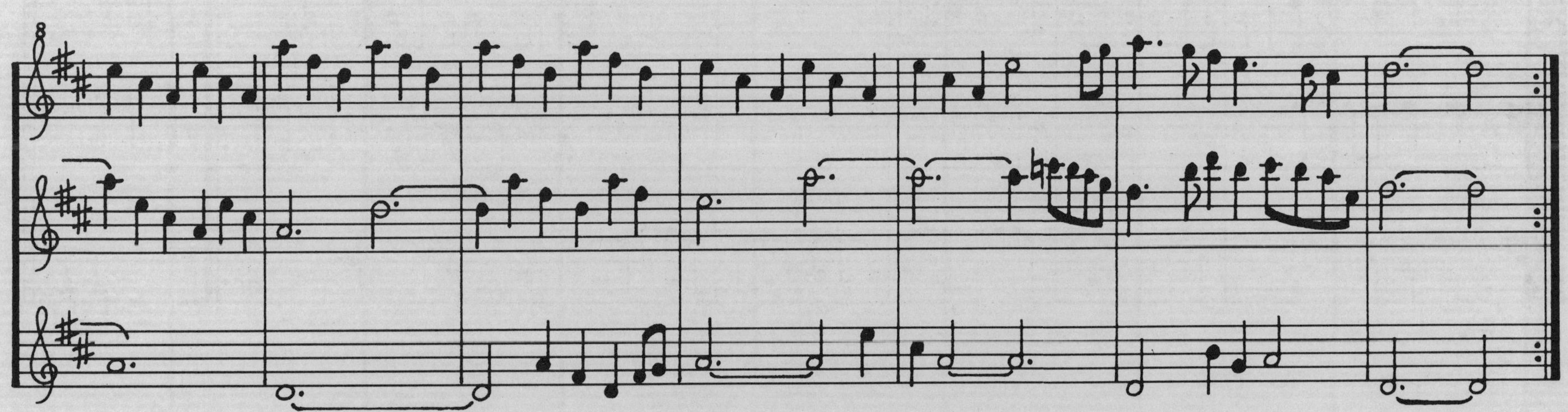

2. THE PARSON AMONG THE PEAS

D'Urfey, *Pills to Purge Melancholy*

NOTE: Tenor recorder-players without the lower double-holes (or keys) for E-flat and C-sharp are advised to play the small notes written where these notes occur, in this and in nos. 5 and 6; unfortunately in one piece ("Hole in the Wall") it was not possible to substitute another note for the E-flats; there is a fingering for this note, for which one must use lower wind pressure and pray for the best: 

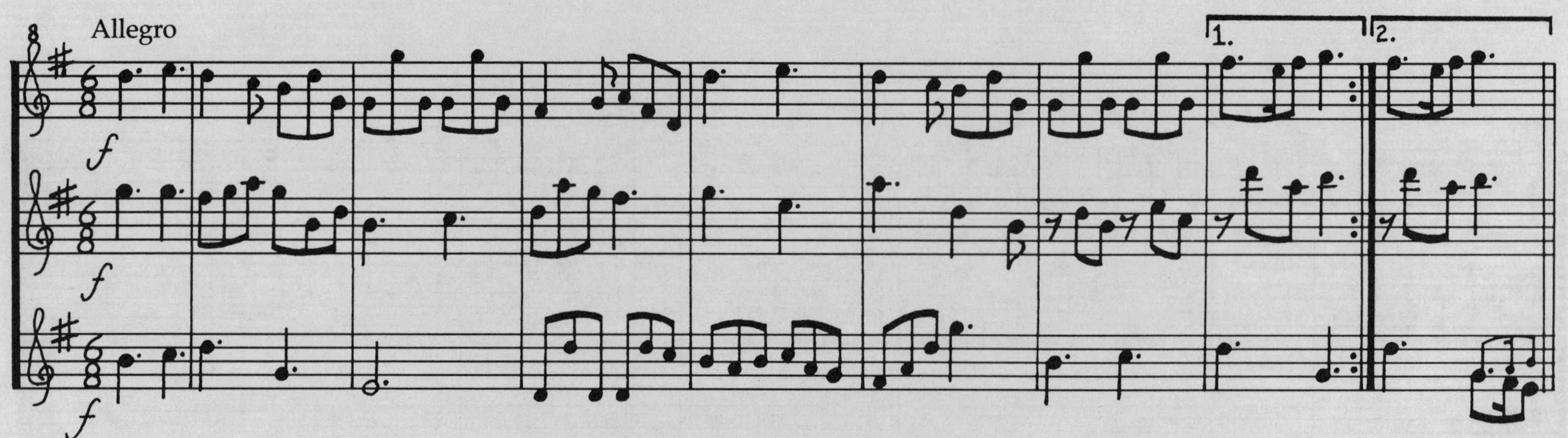

3. DRIVE THE COLD WINTER AWAY

Playford, *Dancing-Master*

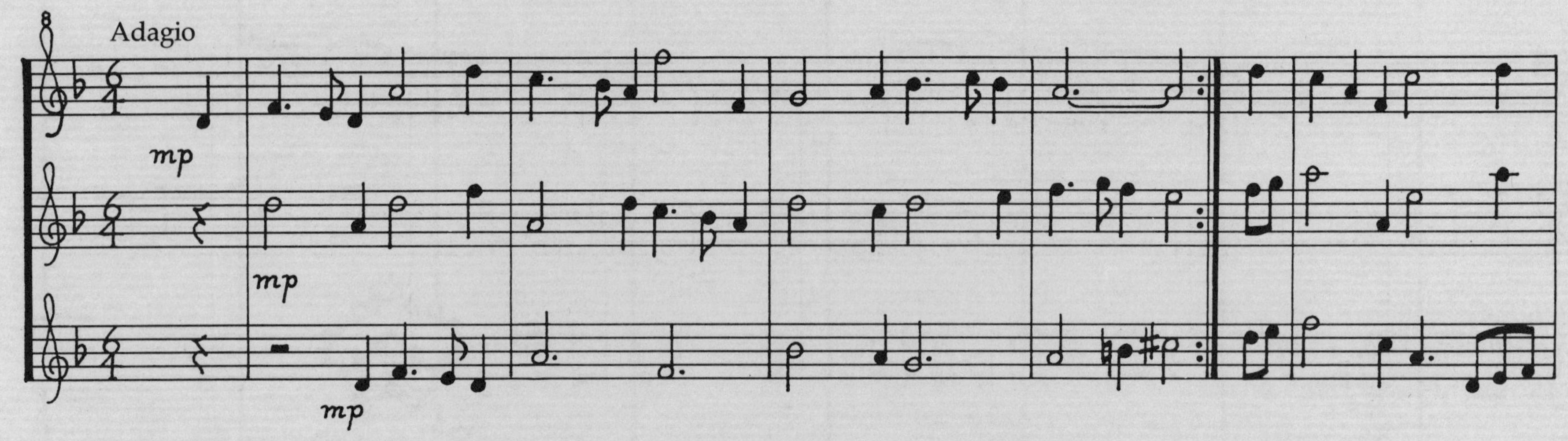

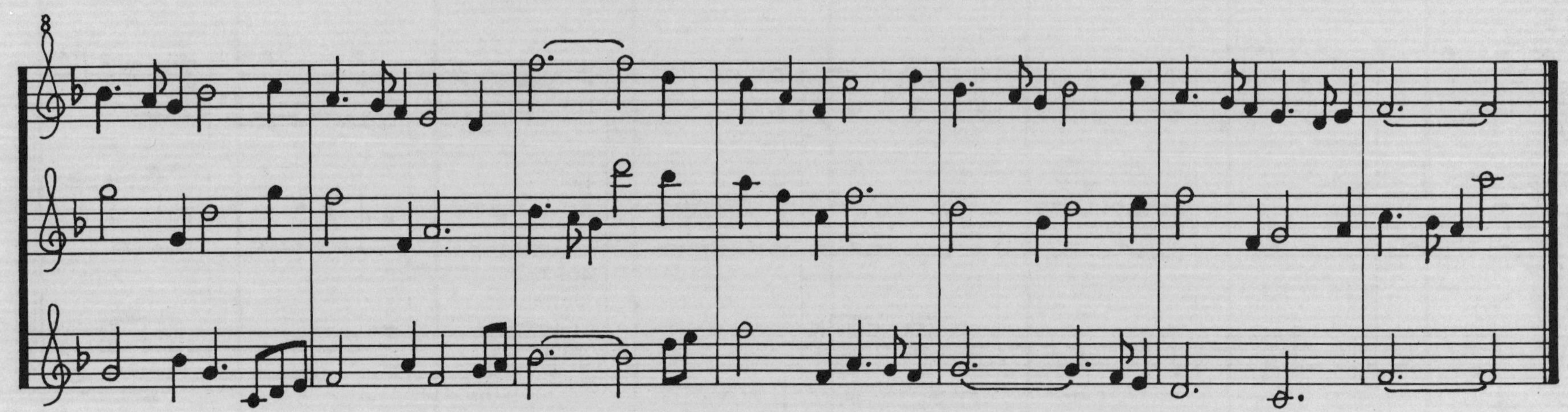

4. THE COUNTRY FARMER'S DAUGHTER

Playford, *Dancing-Master*

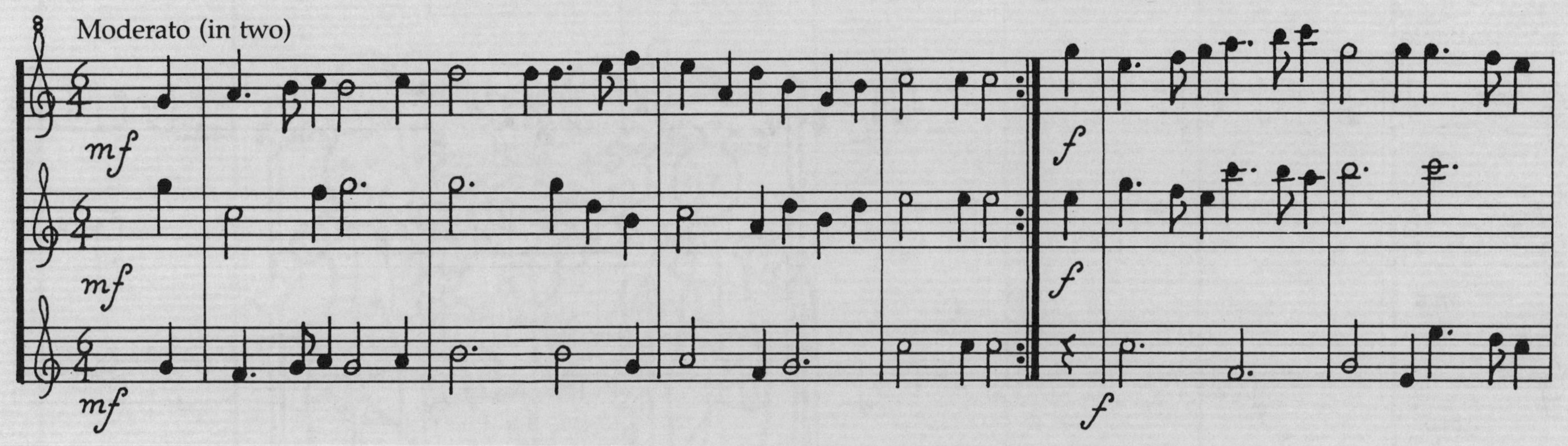

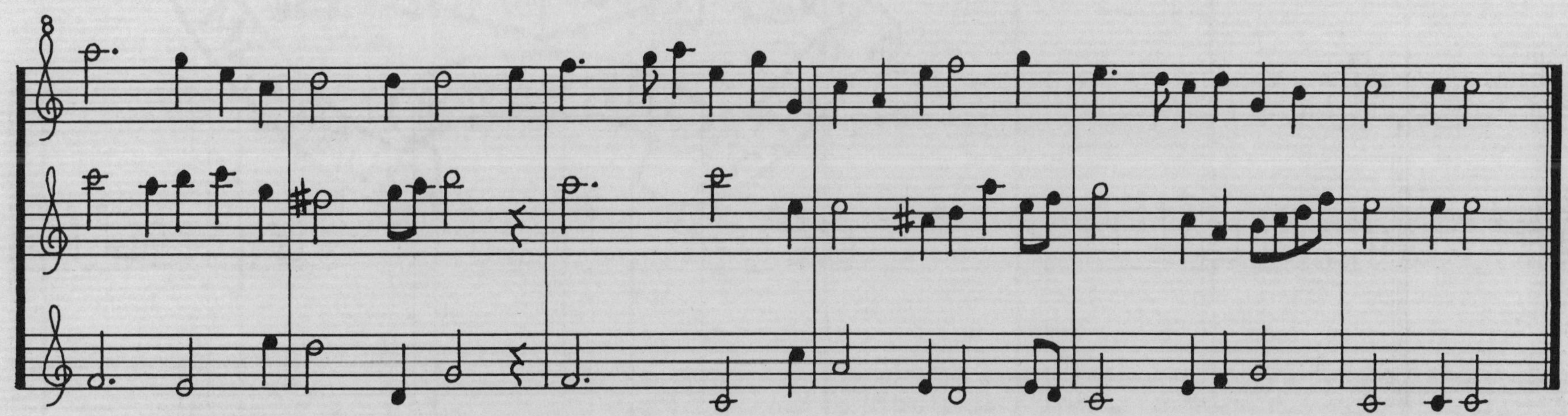

5. THE LASS OF PATIE'S MILL

Gay, *The Beggar's Opera*

Adagio

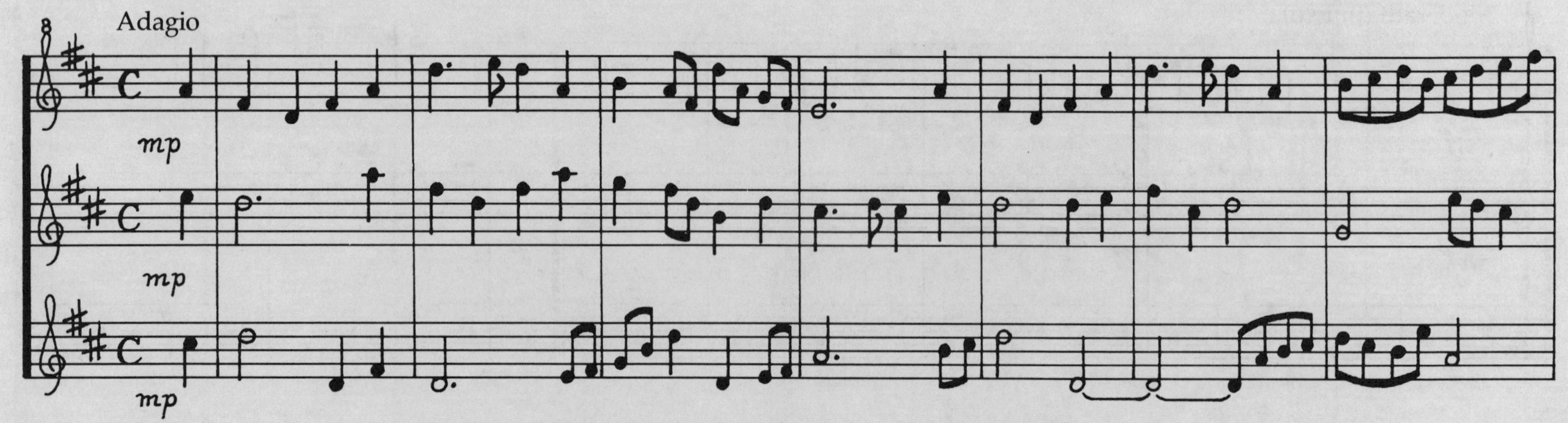

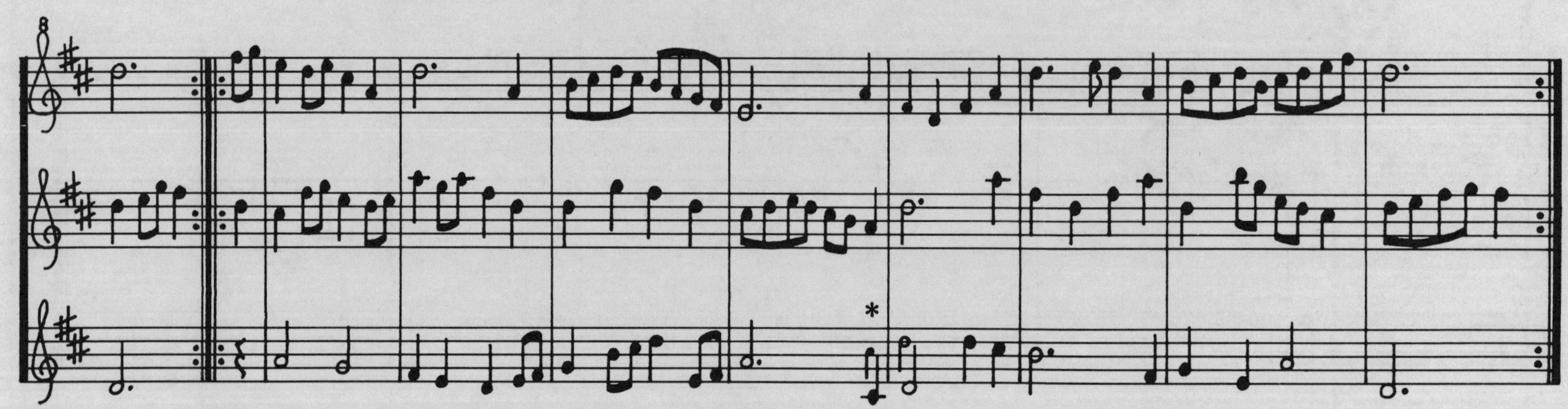

* See p. 2

6. WOU'D YOU HAVE A YOUNG VIRGIN

Gay, *The Beggar's Opera*

Allegretto

* See p. 2

7. HOLE IN THE WALL

Playford, Dancing-Master

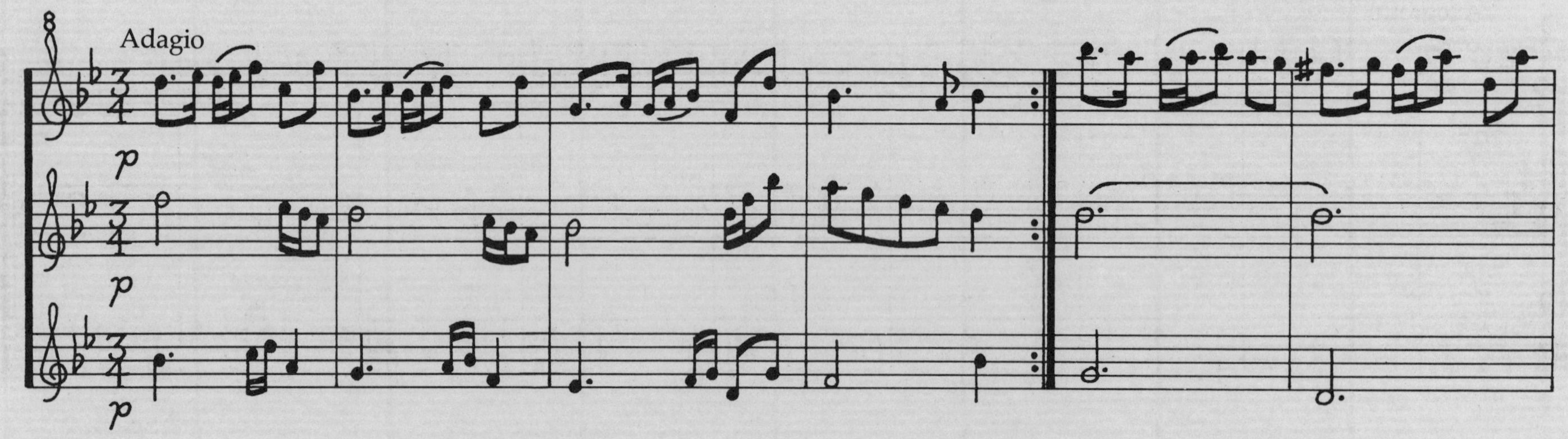

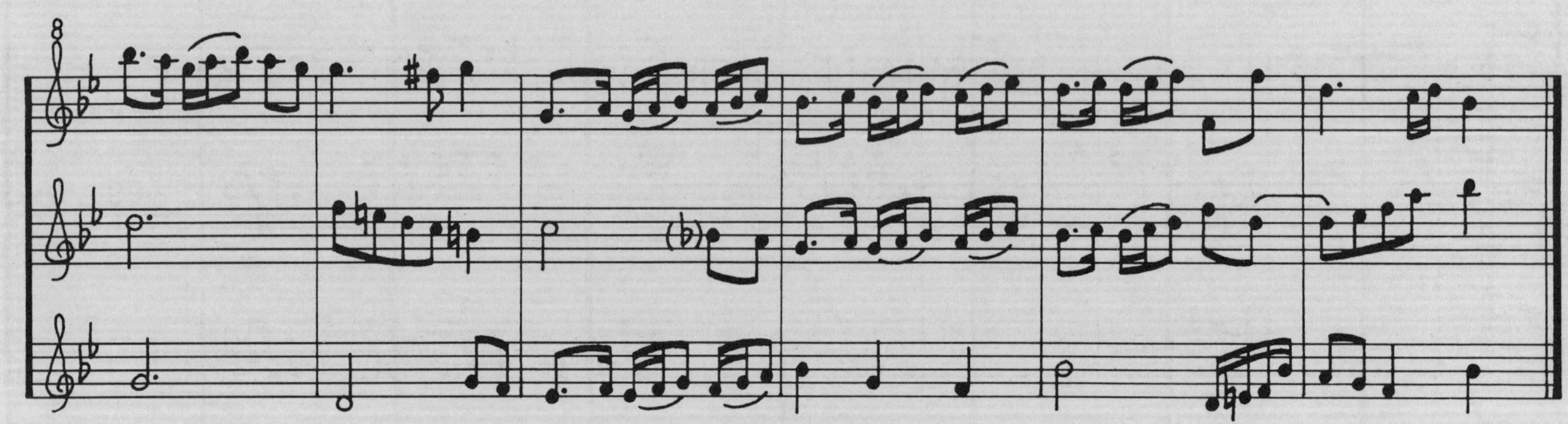

8. AMARYLLIS

Playford, Dancing-Master

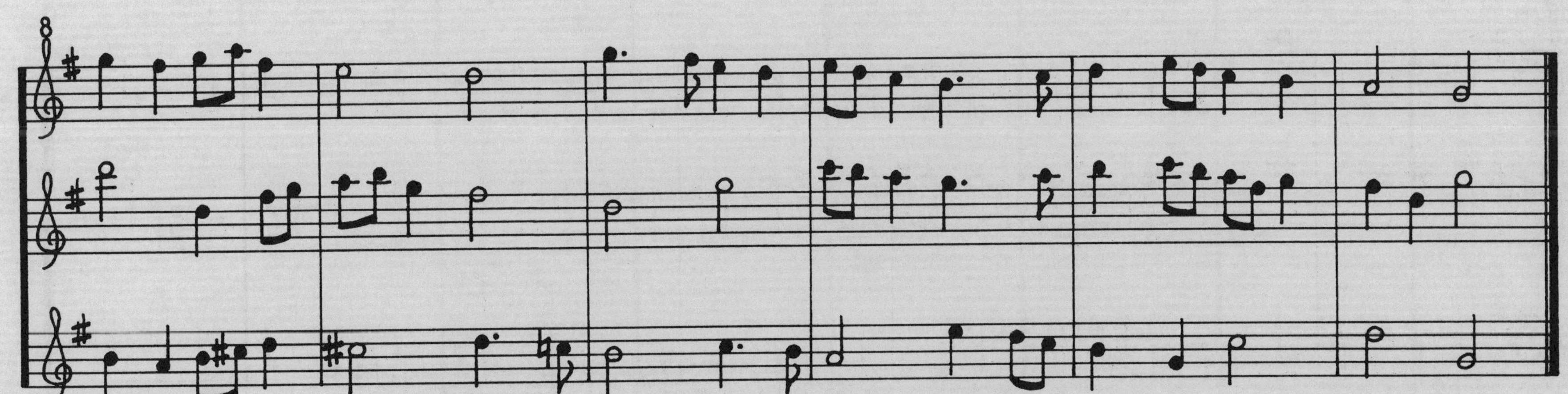

9. JOAN'S PLACKET

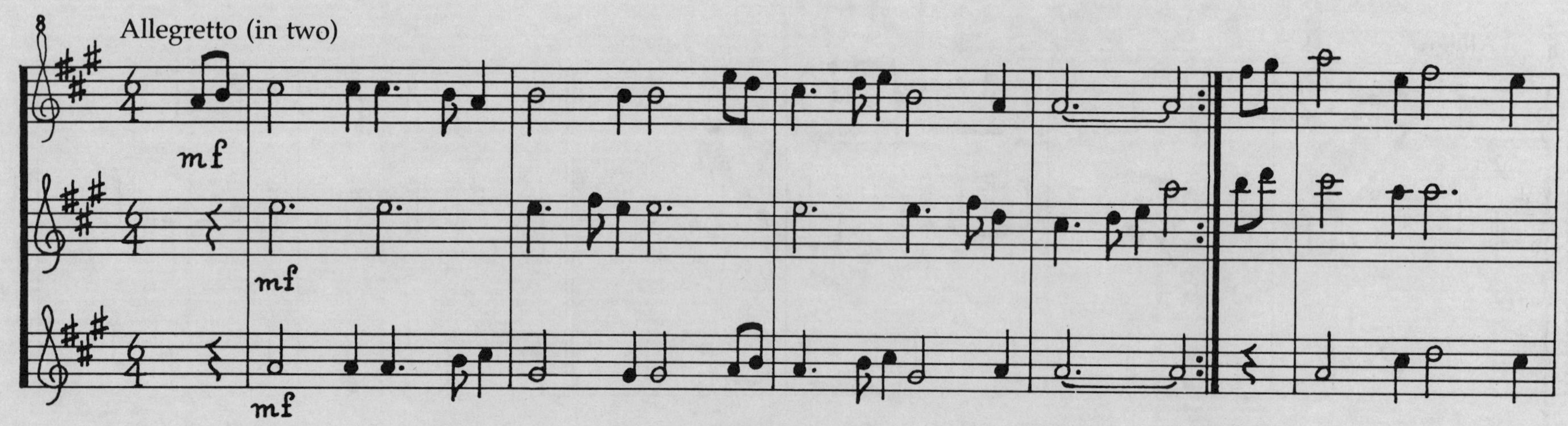

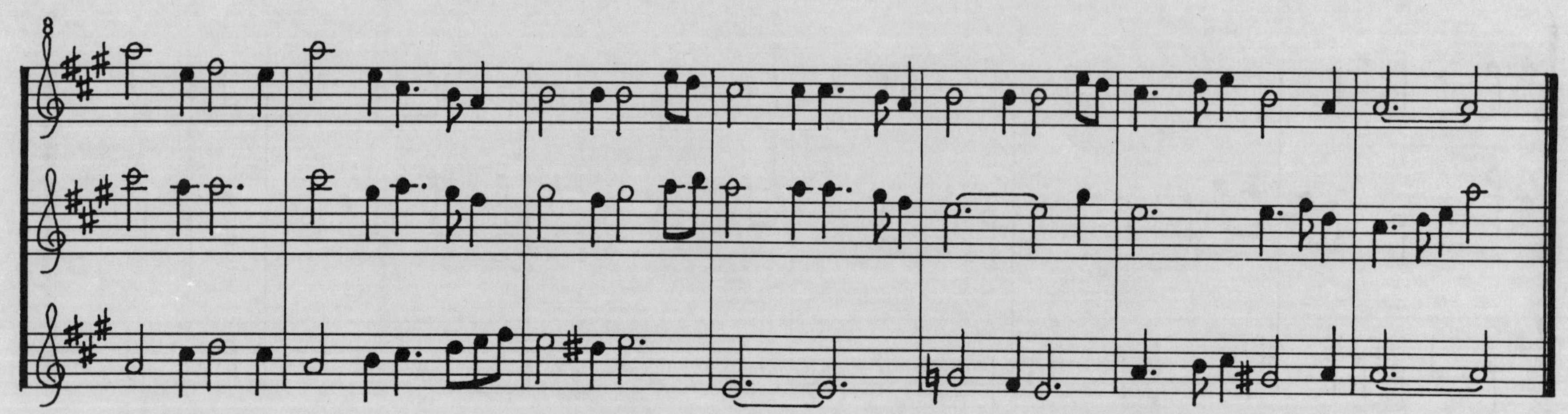

10. PACKINGTON'S POUND

Gay, The Beggar's Opera

11. THE MERRY MILK MAIDS IN GREEN

Playford, Dancing-Master

12. FAREWEL TO LOCHABER

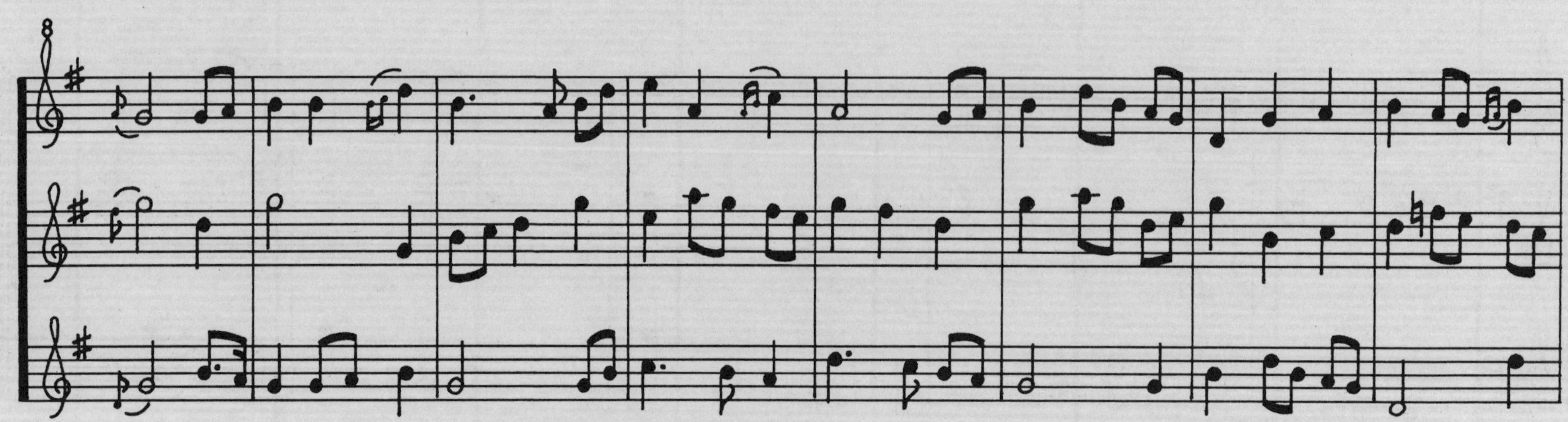

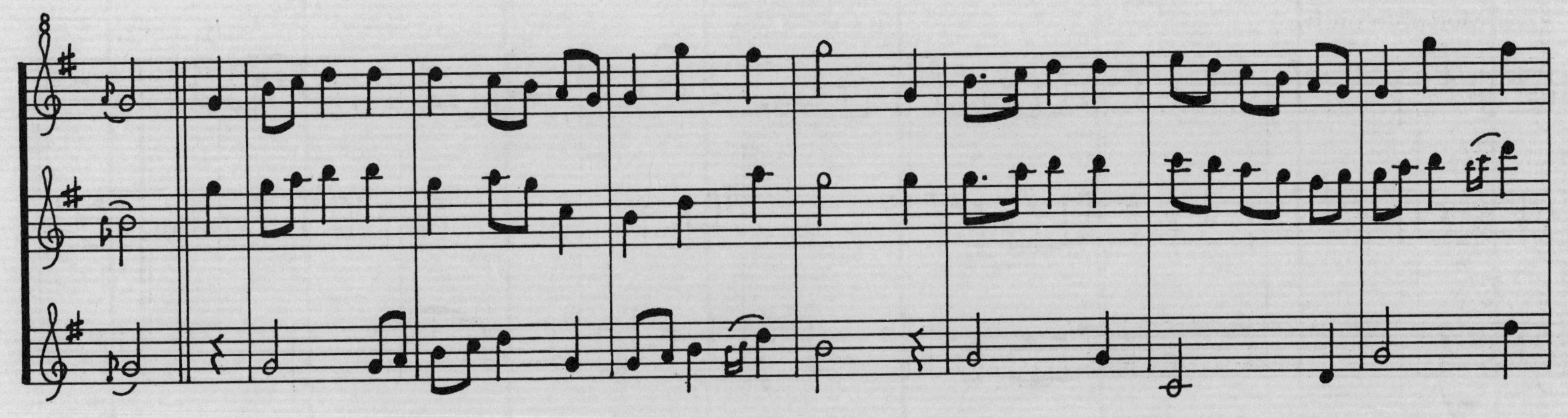

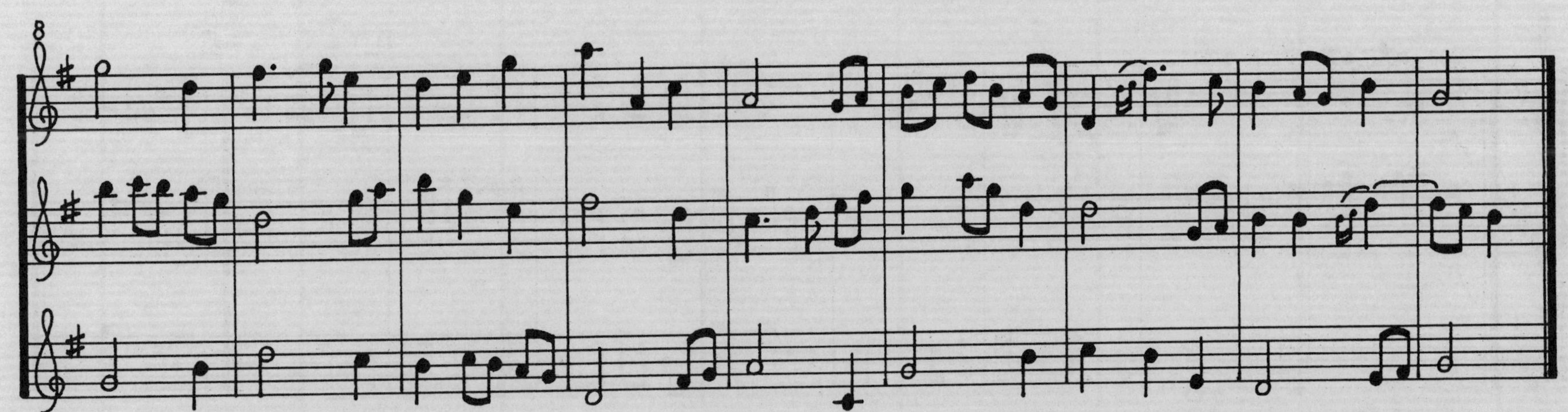

13. LAMBETH WELLS

Playford, *Dancing-Master*

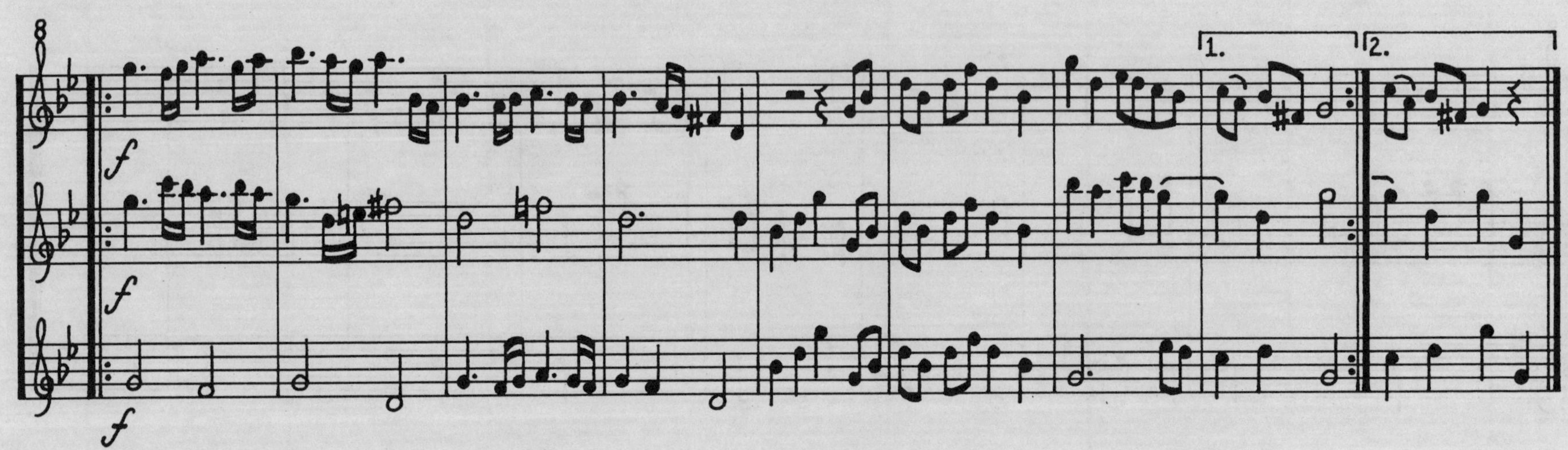